BASICS

ROOF CONSTRUCTION

\\\ TANJA BROTRÜCK

BASICS

ROOF CONSTRUCTION

BIRKHÄUSER – PUBLISHERS FOR ARCHITECTURE
BASEL·BOSTON·BERLIN

CONTENTS

FOREWORD

The roof over our heads satisfies a fundamental human need – it protects us from rain, wind and cold. In addition to these technical requirements it must transfer loads and provide stability: a roof has a variety of functions to fulfil. Craft traditions have generated numerous roof shapes and typologies to address these tasks in a number of ways, which are still used today.

The roof must be aesthetically satisfying as well; it is often called the fifth façade. Variants on flat and pitched roof forms define the character of whole man-made landscapes, and also offer essential stylistic resources for new buildings.

The "Basics" series of books aims to provide instructive and practical explanations for students who are approaching a subject or discipline for the very first time. It presents content with easily comprehensible introductions and examples. The most important principles are systematically elaborated and treated in depth in each volume. Instead of compiling an extensive compendium of specialist knowledge, the series aims to provide an initial introduction to a subject and give readers the necessary expertise for skilled implementation.

The "Roof" volume is aimed at students who are encountering roofs for the first time as part of their training as architects, structural engineers, or other construction professionals. It explains roof types, how construction methods meet structural requirements, and their various advantages and disadvantages. The book gives a clear account of the individual structural elements and layers, and provides guidance on addressing them at the planning stage. It deals with the essential roof structure, insulation and waterproofing, coverings and surfaces, and the basic elements of drainage. The aim is to familiarize students with the necessary technical terms, so that they can translate general facts and differences into concrete design and construction.

Bert Bielefeld, Editor

INTRODUCTION

The roof is part of a building's outer skin, and fulfils a range of functions: first, it protects the space below it, open or closed, from the weather. Here the most important aspects are draining precipitation effectively, providing protection from sun and wind, and affording privacy.

Different structures can be used according to functional requirements or the design approach. The roofs described in this book demonstrate basic principles. They form a basis for new roof planning approaches, which are in a constant state of development.

Various forces act on the roof. They must be conducted to the ground directly, or via outside walls, columns or foundations.

We distinguish between various structures and roof forms. A number of factors are involved in choosing a suitable roof. Appearance is probably the most important criterion. Then come the configuration and size of the plan view; construction costs and relevant building regulations play a crucial role.

〉📖 The choice of structure and materials should be appropriate to the project in hand: elaborate prefabricated steel constructions are rarely used for private houses, and hand-finished on-site detailing is avoided for industrial buildings where possible.

Typically regional roof forms often emerge. Alpine regions usually have shallow-pitched roofs with very large overhangs, while houses with

📖
\\Hint:
Roof pitch and roof shapes are often stipulated
for building plots subject to a new master
plan. If the plot is in a developed area and
there is no master plan, "fitting in with
the surroundings" is the correct approach
to building regulations. The local building
department will provide information about
whether a particular site is subject to precise
stipulations.

steeply pitched roofs set gable-on to the street > see chapter Roof types are more usual in northern European coastal regions. But buildings' functions have also produced typical roof shapes. For example, indoor tennis courts have vaulted barrel roofs that follow the flight of the ball, while normal events halls have flat roofs to facilitate flexible use.

Different roof types can be combined, but this often produces a complicated geometry of details. Simple structures are therefore preferable, to avoid leakage.

The main distinction in roof types is between pitched and flat roofs; generally speaking a roof is considered pitched if it inclines by more than 5°. These two roof forms are clearly distinct in structure and function, and will be considered separately in this book.

LOADS AND FORCES

The statics of a building deal with its structural stability: the forces acting on it and their effects have to be calculated. Newton's law says: force = mass × acceleration. As a rule, forces cannot be identified directly, but only indirectly, by their effects. For example, if we observe the acceleration of a body, we will establish that one or more forces are at work. But in building, statics is the theory of the equilibrium of forces: the various parts of the buildings should be at rest. It is also essential to ensure that the internal forces are also in equilibrium, which means that each component part has to withstand load. Its ability to do this depends on its thickness or dimensions, and on the solidity and elasticity of the material.

If a load compresses a construction element, compressive forces are generated. If the forces affecting the element are pulling it apart, tensile forces are generated. If opposing forces affect an element at different points, the element tries to twist. The building industry applies the technical term momentum or torque to this torsion. The sum of the maximum forces that could be exerted identifies the overall forces that have to be directed into the construction below and absorbed by it.

The forces affecting a building or a construction element are also defined according to their direction. A distinction is made between longitudinal forces and lateral forces.

Various forces act on buildings. They must be identified at the planning stage and plans must be made for transferring them into the

Type of load		Duration	Main direction	Determination
Dead load		Permanent	Vertical	Calculated according to the quantity and specific weights of the structural elements (in KN/m^2)
Imposed load		Variable	Vertical	Can be taken from table values as a mean values for certain uses (in KN/m^2)
Snow and ice load		Variable	Vertical	Can be taken from table values according to the roof pitch and snow-loaded areas
Wind load		Variable	Variable	Can be taken from table values according to the roof pitch and wind-loaded areas

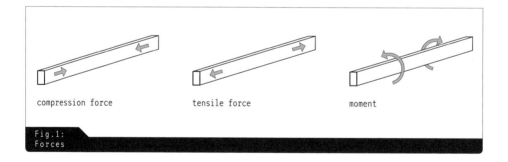

compression force   tensile force   moment

Fig.1:
Forces

ground. Loads can act horizontally, in longitudinal and transverse directions, and vertically. Identifying the individual loads forms the basis for dimensioning the roof construction. Planners must first decide which materials to use, so that the building's self-weight can be determined. The <u>dead load</u> is a permanent load. It acts vertically downwards. <u>Imposed loads</u> are the next factor. These can be movable objects, such as furniture, or people. But it is not necessary to list every object individually and take it into account when dimensioning the structure. Mean values are available for different types, e.g. dwellings, factories and warehouses. Individual specifications are required only in exceptional cases. If a structural element is not planned to be generally accessible, a diagonal roof section, for example, it is still necessary to ensure that a person could walk on it for maintenance purposes, or during the assembly process. This is known as a point load. As a rule, imposed loads act vertically downwards, like a dead load.

<u>Wind,</u> <u>snow</u> and <u>ice</u> loads act on the roof from the outside. Snow and ice exert pressure on the roof because of their weight, and so also create vertical forces, but wind can act both horizontally and vertically. These forces are identified as wind suction and wind pressure. Wind suction acts as a lifting force. Structural elements that are so loaded must be appropriately protected against being blown away.

\\Tip:
Individual national standards provide load compilation tables. The individual weights of materials and structural elements and assumptions about imposed, snow and wind loads can be taken from these. The most important standards are listed in the appendix to this book.

PITCHED ROOFS

BASICS

By far the most roofs for detached dwellings are pitched. Pitched roofs are exceptionally well suited to draining precipitation off buildings. The loadbearing structure is usually of wood and is made by hand, although steel and concrete are also possible. The triangular cross sections under the roof surfaces absorb horizontal wind forces well and conduct them into the structure.

The highest point of the roof is known as the <u>ridge</u>, and the lower edges as the <u>eaves</u>. The diagonal link on the wall of the house, at the <u>gable</u>, forms the <u>verge</u>. › see Fig. 2 When two roof surfaces intersect, the intersection line pointing outwards is known as the <u>arris</u> and the internal line as the <u>valley</u>. It the roof is set on a wall that rises higher than the topmost ceiling in the house, this wall is called a <u>jamb wall</u>. The <u>roof pitch</u> is defined by the angle between the roof surface and the horizontal. This dimension is always given as the inside angle and is measured in degrees. For gutters and waterproofing elements the term slope is used. This is usually given as a percentage.

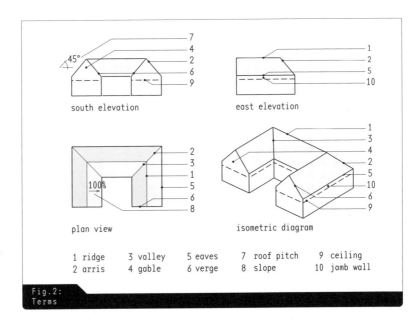

south elevation

east elevation

plan view

isometric diagram

1 ridge	3 valley	5 eaves	7 roof pitch	9 ceiling
2 arris	4 gable	6 verge	8 slope	10 jamb wall

Fig. 2:
Terms

Fig.3:
Monopitch roof – Gable roof – Mansard roof – Hipped roof

ROOF TYPES

The different roof forms have names that define the nature of the roof and gable pitch.

Monopitch roof

A single inclined area is called a monopitch roof. This form produces walls of different height at the ridge and eaves, so is particularly suitable if a building is intended to face in a particular direction, e.g. towards the garden (for dwellings) or towards the street (for prominent public buildings).

Gable roof

Two juxtaposed inclined planes form a gable roof. This and the monopitch roof are the simplest pitched roof forms.

Mansard roof

A mansard roof has two juxtaposed roof planes of different pitches, and is now less commonly used. It was intended to give more headroom if the roof space were to be used.

If the end wall under the pitched roof areas is upright, it forms a gable. If this area faces a street or square, the building can is said to stand gable-on to the street. The opposite, eaves-on, is less common.

Hipped roof

If the roof slopes on all four sides it is known as a hipped roof.

Pavilion roof

A pavilion roof has all its roof planes pitched, with outside walls of equal length. The roof planes meet at a single point.

Half-hipped roof

If a roof has a gable and a pitched roof plane on the end wall, it is known as a half-hip.

Barrel roof

Roofs can be built with cylindrical vaulting, as a barrel roof. Roofs that are curved on all sides are domes.

Shed roof

Shed roofs have small monopitch roofs or gable roofs aligned like the teeth of a saw; the steeper plane is usually glazed. Fully glazed versions are common. They are often used to light large spaces such as production halls.

14

Fig.4:
Pavilion roof – Half-hipped roof – Barrel roof – Shed roof

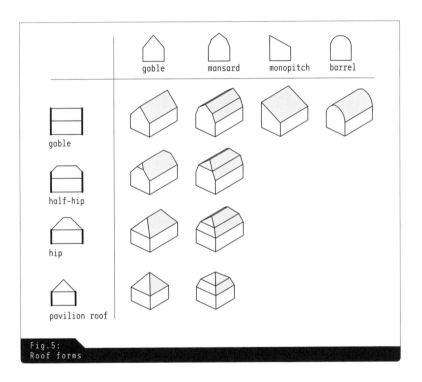

Fig.5:
Roof forms

\\Hint:
The term headroom defines the height of a space that people can use comfortably. An area is considered fully usable if it has a clear headroom of 2.2 m.

\\Hint:
When calculating the useful area of attic storeys, only half of any area 1 to 2 m high is counted. Areas 2 m and higher are counted in full, and areas under 1 m high are omitted altogether. Area calculations stipulations are derived from the individual national standards and areas where they apply.

15

The terms explained here are sometimes combined to describe a roof form fully, for example a hipped mansard roof. If the building has only one gable, this is not defined separately. The simple terms gable, mansard or monopitch roof are retained.

DORMERS

Dormers are also basic roof forms. They are used to light the roof space, or as an exterior design feature, providing additional usable space in the attic area. Note that far less incident light is admitted by the diagonal configuration of roof and dormer than by a window in a vertical wall. It is preferable to place windows in the gable walls. Dormer width should be restricted to one to two rafter fields. › see chapter Roof structures Additional loadbearing elements may also be needed for the window; they can be tied into the frame. Note that the dormer pitch should not be less than the minimum roof pitch prescribed for the roof covering. › see chapter Roof coverings All dormer surfaces must satisfy the same requirements of density, moisture, thermal insulation etc. as the roof itself.

Dustpan dormer

The form of the dormer depends on the roof covering. A dustpan dormer roof slopes less steeply than the main roof. Triangular vertical surfaces are created at the sides.

Gable dormer

A gable dormer also has vertical triangular areas, but meets the main roof at valleys, producing a street-facing gable roof.

Triangular dormer

The term triangular dormer is used only when there is a triangular gable plane.

Eyebrow dormer

The eyebrow rises out of the roof in a shallow arc. The roof plane is not interrupted. An eyebrow dormer is roughly ten times as wide as it is high. It requires the same roof height as a dustpan dormer.

Fig.6:
Dustpan dormer – Gable dormer – Triangular dormer

Fig.7:
Eyebrow dormer – Bull's eye – Barrel dormer

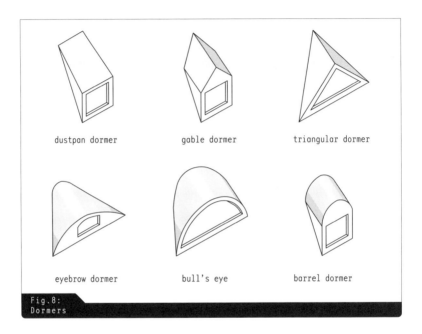

dustpan dormer   gable dormer   triangular dormer

eyebrow dormer   bull's eye   barrel dormer

Fig.8:
Dormers

Bull's eye

The bull's eye forms a semicircle in the gable area. It can be fitted into various kinds of roof covering, but the circular shape requires a covering in sheet metal or some other flexible material.

Barrel dormer

If the semicircle is placed on a straight vertical area, the term barrel dormer is used.

Fig.9:
Wooden loadbearing structures

ROOF STRUCTURES

As well as roof forms, we distinguish between different roof constructions. For smaller roofs, intended for private houses, for example, wood is still the pre-eminent material. It absorbs compression and tensile forces well, and is reasonably priced and easy to work with on site. Loadbearing structures in steel or prestressed concrete beams are used when larger spans are involved; they can also be adopted for domestic building to achieve a particular design effect.

There are three basic loadbearing systems for pitched roofs: couple roof, collar roof and purlin roof.

Couple roof

The couple roof is a simple triple frame form: if the structure is viewed in cross section it consists of two beams leaning against each other, the <u>rafters</u>, connected to the floor below or to a <u>tie beam</u> to form a triangle. This triangular framework is called a pair of rafters. The beams are securely fixed at the connection points, but can turn freely, which is why such a frame is said to be hinged. A couple roof consists of several pairs of rafters in a row. They should be 70 to 80 cm apart, up to a maximum of 90 cm. The rafters are subject to loads from self-weight, snow etc. › see chapter Loads The tie beam linking them absorbs the tensile forces that are trying to pull the pair of rafters apart. Hence the connection between the rafters and the tie beam or ceiling must allow the forces generated to be transferred into the wall or supporting member below. In the traditional craft design, the tie beam projects beyond the triangular frame at the eaves. This projec-

Verge member tion is called the <u>verge member</u>.

19

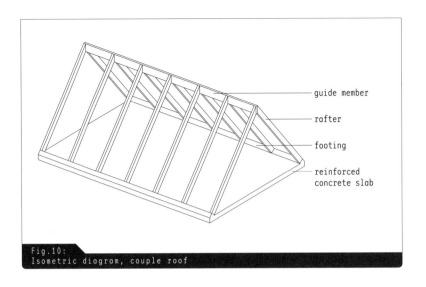

guide member

rafter

footing

reinforced
concrete slab

Fig.10:
Isometric diagram, couple roof

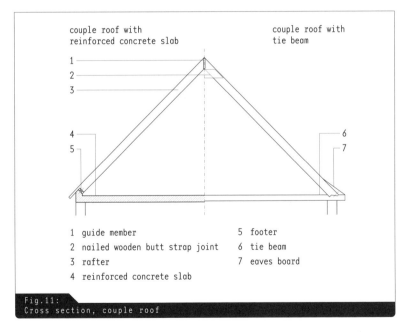

couple roof with
reinforced concrete slab

couple roof with
tie beam

1
2
3

4
5

6
7

1 guide member
2 nailed wooden butt strap joint
3 rafter
4 reinforced concrete slab

5 footer
6 tie beam
7 eaves board

Fig.11:
Cross section, couple roof

Eaves board

The verge member will generally be more than 20 cm long. The roof
pitch has to be extended here by adding an <u>eaves board</u> so that the roof
covering can run out through the wall at the end of the building. This produces a curb or kink in the roof surface, and alters the pitch.

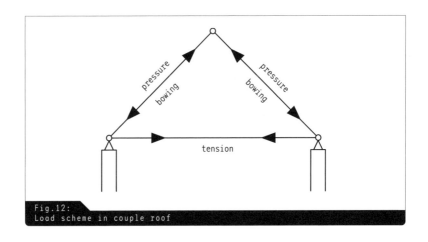

Fig.12:
Load scheme in couple roof

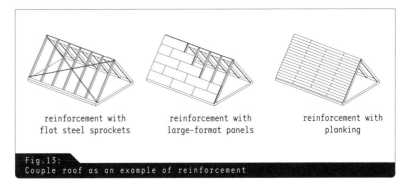

reinforcement with   reinforcement with   reinforcement with
flat steel sprockets   large-format panels   planking

Fig.13:
Couple roof as an example of reinforcement

Nowadays, a projecting roof more commonly uses a ring beam, generally in concrete. Here, a spandrel beam or a floor bevel transfers the diagonal forces from the rafters into the ring beam.

Guide member

A <u>guide member</u> is commonly placed at the ridge joint to facilitate fitting the rafters. This links the rafters longitudinally, but the roof has to be sufficiently reinforced to take longitudinal forces. This can be achieved by fitting wooden sprockets or flat metal strips attached diagonally to the rafters, or by adding flat boarding.

Couple roofs may have a pitch of approx. 25 to 50°. They are suitable for spans of up to 8 m, as otherwise the requisite timber cross sections would not be economically viable. They tend to be used when column-free plan views are required, as all the loads are transferred via the longitudinal walls. They are only moderately suitable for installing special elements such as dormer windows or large areas of roof windows and the associated trimmers. > see chapter Trimming

Collar roof

Collar roof

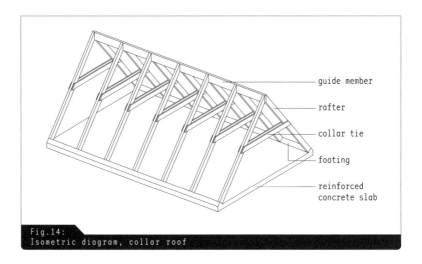

The collar roof, like the couple roof, is a triangular framework. Bowing of the rafters is reduced by an arrangement of horizontal ties, the collar ties, so that greater spans can be bridged. For structural reasons, the collar ties are usually arranged in pairs, as horizontal ties, and fixed to the sides of the rafters. They are best positioned statically in the middle of the rafter. The collar ties can also be arranged at a height 65 to 75 percent of the total roof height to make the roof space accessible and provide more headroom. The design of ridge and eaves points and longitudinal reinforcement can be treated in the same way as for couple roofs.

Collar roofs are most economical at a roof pitch of more than 45°, and are suitable for spans of 10–15 m.

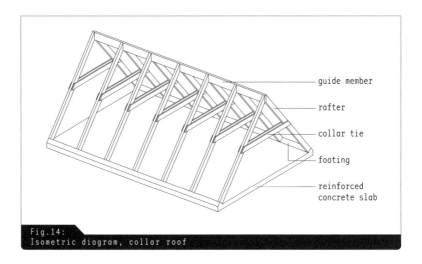

guide member

rafter

collar tie

footing

reinforced concrete slab

Fig.14:
Isometric diagram, collar roof

\\Hint:
A span defines the length bridged by an
unsupported structural element. For couple and
collar roofs this is the width of the building.

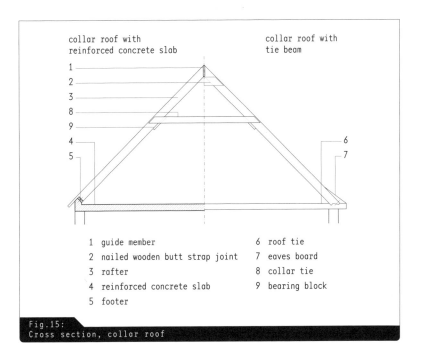

collar roof with   collar roof with
reinforced concrete slab tie beam

1 guide member   6 roof tie
2 nailed wooden butt strap joint 7 eaves board
3 rafter   8 collar tie
4 reinforced concrete slab   9 bearing block
5 footer

Fig.15:
Cross section, collar roof

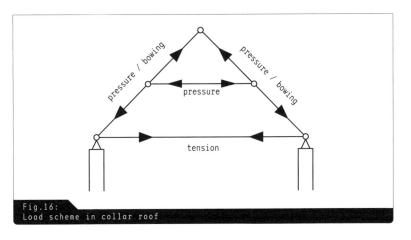

pressure / bowing   pressure / bowing
pressure
tension

Fig.16:
Load scheme in collar roof

Purlin roof

Purlin roof

A purlin roof has horizontal members – purlins – supporting the rafters. The purlins can be supported by the outside walls or by uprights, the

Post

posts, or stays. Rafters are subject to bending loads, which are transferred

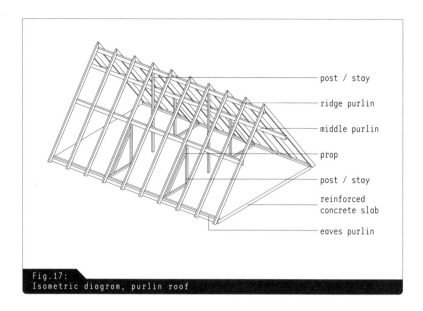

Fig.17:
Isometric diagram, purlin roof

post / stay
ridge purlin
middle purlin
prop
post / stay
reinforced
concrete slab
eaves purlin

Props

to the purlins. The posts have to be braced so that they can also absorb horizontal wind loads. The <u>props</u> run parallel to the roof pitch, with a space between them and the rafters. They are attached to the sides of the posts and make the roof better able to absorb transverse forces.

The basic form is the simple purlin roof. Here, the rafters are placed on the ridge purlin (at the ridge) and the eaves purlin (at the eaves). Loads in the ridge purlin area are transferred through posts. This simple support structure gives the expression <u>simple</u>, or single, <u>purlin roof</u>. In a double purlin roof, the rafters are supported by the eaves purlin and a central purlin (preferably in the middle of the eaves). As the span of the rafters is shortened, they are less liking to sag. Collar ties can be used for transverse reinforcement. If the ground plan is particularly large, a triple purlin roof can be constructed with eaves, centre and ridge purlins.

The purlin roof is the most versatile classical roof structure form. The rafter system is independent, and a wide variety of irregular and composite roofs can be constructed. Chimneys and windows can easily be fitted by trimming. > see chapter Trimming

Roof pitch can be selected at will for purlin roofs. Good rafter lengths are up to 4.5 m between the purlins.

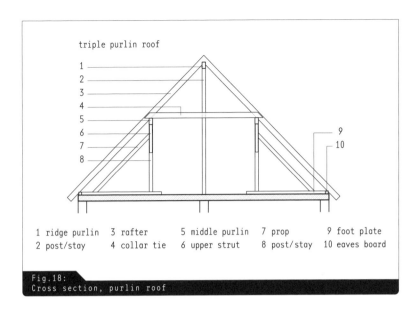

triple purlin roof

1 ridge purlin	3 rafter	5 middle purlin	7 prop	9 foot plate
2 post/stay	4 collar tie	6 upper strut	8 post/stay	10 eaves board

Fig.18:
Cross section, purlin roof

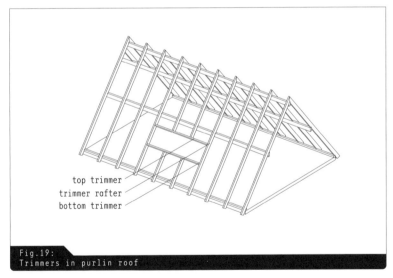

top trimmer
trimmer rafter
bottom trimmer

Fig.19:
Trimmers in purlin roof

It is important when using this structure that the loads from the posts can be transferred into the building's loadbearing system. The posts should be positioned on loadbearing walls, joists or upright members below them.

If the rafters are longer than 7 m there should be a ridge purlin as well as the eaves and centre purlins. This then also transfers forces directed down into the loadbearing walls by upright members. If this is not possible because of the ground plan layout of the floor below, a truss can be deployed. Here, the upright members below the ridge purlin are taken only to collar or horizontal ties, where the vertical loads are transferred horizontally. The triangle of rafters, horizontal ties and uprights then forms a frame comparable with a couple roof.

Truss

Trimming

Trimmers

If the roof space is to be used, larger openings than the spaces between the rafters are sometimes needed to take chimneys up through the roof, for example, or to insert windows. Here, the rafters are interrupted and a trimmer is inserted.

Trimmers are horizontal beams between rafters bridging one or more rafter fields and transferring the loads into the rafters at the sides (trimmer rafters). Ideally the size should be such that the height of the timbers is the same as that of the rafters. Then all the other structural elements can be put in place without needing any compensation in terms of level.

Roof windows and dormers

Roof-lights

The placing of windows in the roof to provide light and ventilation must take account of the way the roof space is used. If roofs are not used but can be walked on, roof-lights are recommended. These are fitted directly into the roof covering. They do not meet any particular requirements in terms of windproofing and heat insulation, but are reasonably priced and usually easy to maintain. As well as providing basic lighting for the indoor area, they make it possible to inspect the roof from the roof space and check the condition of gutters and the roof covering. This is particularly important if it is impossible or very difficult to access the roof with a ladder because the building is too high or awkwardly placed.

Adequate lighting is essential if living or working accommodation has been built into the roof. As a rule, the proportion of window area should be at least one eighth of the ground area. Façade windows in the gable (if there is one), dormer windows, and windows in the roof itself can be used to provide light and ventilation. The advantage of vertical windows in dormers and gables is that they do not easily get dirty, as precipitation does not usually fall directly onto the surface of the glass. At the same time, it is possible to come right up to the windows and so enjoy a better

> ◍

view of the surroundings. Concerning possible fire escapes routes, care
should be taken that roof windows can also be used as a "second escape
route" (the first is down a staircase). It case of fire it is essential that the
roof windows are large enough, and that people in the roof space can at-
tract attention to themselves.

For roof space ventilation, care should be taken at the planning stage
to allow for the fact that that heat will rise. If the roof space is open to the
ridge, measures should be taken to ensure that hot air can escape from the
upper roof area.

Windows in the
roof

Windows built into the surface of the roof itself are now usually
installed by the roofing contractor as prefabricated elements. All the connecting parts in the various makes are available for different coverings
and rooftop fittings. The products available conform to the usual distances
between rafters (between 70 and 90 cm). Roof windows can be installed
between two rafters, or in one rafter field, or can extend over several rafter
fields, in which case a trimmer must be fitted. › see chapter Trimming If rows of
windows are needed, combination covering frames are available that en-
able several windows to be arranged next to each other without trimmers.
The height of the windows is restricted to approx. 1.6 m, as otherwise it is
impracticable to open or close them, and they weigh too much. If a larger
area has to be fitted with windows, two can be installed, one above the
other. The top edge of the windows should be at least 1.9 m, so that it is
possible to look out. The parapet height is usually between 0.85 and 1 m.
A higher parapet could be used for kitchens and bathrooms. The lower the
roof pitch, the greater the area of window needed to achieve the necessary
height. When planning roof windows, care should be taken not to break the
ventilation cross section inside the roof structure. The air must be able to

circulate freely around the window. Sheeting strips must be attached to the windows on all sides, and any water must be able to flow away unimpeded (e.g. by installing a wedge above the window). The heat insulation must be taken right up to the roof window and the gaps must be completely filled with insulation. The vapour barrier must also be attached on all sides, so that atmospheric moisture in the room cannot penetrate the insulation.

We distinguish between various opening methods for roof windows. A swing window is fixed in the middle at the sides. When opening it, the upper half swings into the roof space, while the lower rises outside it. A hinged window is fixed at the top edge and the whole window folds upwards and outwards. As it is very hard to clean the outside of such windows (by reaching around the window), combined folding and swing windows are often used. Hinged windows are also offered with sliding functions. Here, the window is pushed away to the side so that it then lies above the surface of the roof. Such windows are very elaborate and expensive, and so seldom used.

Care must be taken when fitting roof windows to leave sufficient distance between the windows and the adjacent buildings or boundaries. Building regulations lay down that roof windows must be approx. 1.25 m from firewalls. For terraced houses set gable-on to the street, › see chapter Roof types the windows must be at least 2 m from the eaves. Roof windows are often used when building regulations do not permit dormers.

Dormers

Lighting the roof space with dormers creates additional usable space, because they allow more headroom. The interior height under the dormer must be at least 2 m. Just as for roof windows, the parapet height is between 0.85 and 1 m. Small dormers can be placed above a rafter field, and are then the same width (approx. 70 to 80 cm). Trimmers have to be used for wider dormers. For couple roofs, this is usually possible only if the dormer width is restricted to two rafter fields. The rafters in purlin roofs can be interrupted in several fields. The forces from the rafters are then transferred into the ceiling vertically.

The front of the dormer is made from a squared timber frame, known as a dormer truss. It is placed either on the rafters or directly on the intermediate floor. If the dormer truss is placed on the intermediate floor, the roof space between the dormer truss and the eaves is usually sealed off and concludes the space. For shed dormers the key rafter is placed directly above the trimmer rafter. It is then supported by the dormer truss at the dormer end. The side triangle is called the dormer cheek. This area is usually reinforced with rough tongue-and-groove sheets or some other flat material. The side surfaces of the dormers must be insulated and sealed just like the rest of the roof. The dormer cheeks are usually clad in metal or slate because these materials are good for application to inclined surfaces. It is also possible to glaze the sides of dormers, which provides correspondingly more light.

The width of the dormer is determined by the coverage span of the material concerned. This is calculated from the width x number of pantiles (or other covering material). The equivalent applies to the length of the area removed. › see chapter Roof battens

If time is short, fitting prefabricated dormers is recommended. They can usually be placed on the existing roof within a single day, and the roof can be watertight again within the shortest possible period.

LAYERS OF STRUCTURAL ELEMENTS

Roof coverings
The roof covering's principal function is to allow precipitation to drain away reliably and to prevent moisture penetration from driven snow, for example. Roof covering should be rain- and weatherproof, and also fireproof. They must also guarantee moisture transfer from the inside to the outside, and protect the structural elements underneath them from the wind. Key features in the choice of a suitable covering are design, and then the roof pitch and the shape of the roof. Valleys or angles are more easily created with small-format materials such as flat tails. › see section Flat elements Large straight areas of roof are more easily and economically created with pantiles. However, many coverings work only up to a certain minimum roof pitch. The manufacturer's stipulated roof pitch for a particular roofing material always relates to the minimum pitch unless otherwise stated. If this is not reached in some places, water or dust can be prevented from penetrating the structural or insulation course by an underlay. › see section Waterproofing Various types of roof covering material are available, again in different materials.

› 🖿

Thatched roof
One ancient form of covering that is now found only regionally or sporadically is reed or straw thatch. It should be applied at an angle greater than 45°. At an ideal 50° the wind presses the thatch against the substructure and the proportion of lifting force is low. The covering is attached to a framework in several superimposed bundles.

Flat roof covering elements can be in wood (shingles), stone, concrete or clay. The standard roof pitch for shingles depends on the length of the shingles, the overlap for the individual shingles and the number of courses. Simple two-course shingle roofs can be constructed only if the pitch is a minimum of 70°, in other words almost horizontal, while the more elaborate three-course version goes to 22°.

Flat stone elements are usually made of slate. They come in the form of rectangular, acute-angled, scalloped or scale tiles and are pinned to a framework in the overlay area, following individual rules. The standard roof pitch for slate coverings is 25 to 30°.

Concrete or clay tiles are produced industrially. The advantage is that they can be bought to suit specific situations, such as edging or penetrations. An upstand can also be created if the tiles are to be laid on roof lathing. The standard pitch for concrete and clay tiles is between 25 and 40°.

Profiled roof tiles in their various forms are made of clay or concrete. Just like the industrially produced flat tiles, special shapes can be prefabricated for many particular situations. Unlike flat tiles, profiled tiles overlap on three sides.

The oldest profile tile is the under-and-over tile: conical hollow tiles are placed so that they interlock. The upper tile is concave, and takes the water into the lower, convex, tiles, which drain the water into the gutter. They have no rims or ribs. Modern tiles' upstands are shaped to interlock at the top and sides, to prevent water penetration. The standard roof pitch for profiled tiles is 22 to 40° according to type.

There are also profiled tiles, such as corrugated tiles, available in various materials for large-format roof coverings. The fibre-cement

> 0
> \\Hint:
> Precise details about standard roof pitches
> for certain roof coverings can be found in
> more advanced literature, for example in
> "Roof Construction Manual – Pitched Roofs" by
> Eberhard Schunk et al., published by Birkhäuser
> Publishers, or in the manufacturers' details.

Fig.20:
Thatched roofs

Fig.21:
Flat roof coverings: wooden shingles

Fig.22:
Flat roof coverings: slates

Fig.23:
Flat roof coverings: flat tiles

Fig.24:
Roof coverings using profiled tiles

corrugated tile is a simple example. These are laid overlapping on battens, in runs about 1 m wide. Various manufacturers supply versions for edges, intersections and upstands. They can be used for roof pitches of less than 12°. Lower roof pitches are permissible for corrugated bitumen roof coverings. Here, edges or connections are usually constructed using sheet-metal angles.

Industrial construction

Some profiled metal elements can even be used for standard roof pitches of up to 5°. These metal coverings are usually made of galvanized steel, copper or aluminium alloys. They are laid as corrugated profile sheets, following the same principles as fibre cement or bitumen coverings, or as trapezoidal profile sheets. Trapezoidal metal sheets are available in various shapes and sizes. They are made of thin, folded metal sheeting. The edges are optimized in terms of loadbearing properties and can carry loads over long spans. Trapezoidal sheets are supplied as composite sheets with thermal insulation, for industrial construction in particular. The edges of the sheets must overlap and interlock through upstands in order to guarantee the roof's impermeability. They are fixed to the supporting battens with screws, bolts or clips. When working with metal coverings it is important to ensure that no contact corrosion with other metals ensues. A separating course should therefore be placed under the covering ⟩ see chapter Flat roofs, Layers of structural elements if the purlins are made of a different metal, or of concrete.

Strips

Strips are another form of metal covering. They are made of lead, aluminium, copper or stainless or galvanized steel. The strips are usually 500 to 1500 mm wide. They are laid in rows, or courses. The side edges are joined with a welt, a roll or an overlap. The horizontal ends of the sheets are finished with overlaps or transverse welts. Connections to other structural elements or ends are created by hand from turned-over sheet metal. The standard pitch for this kind of roof covering is 5°. Additional precautions are nevertheless recommended for lower pitches.

Roof battens

Flat roof covering materials are fixed to the battens with screws, nails, bolts or clips, but roof tiles with an upstand are laid on battens.

Roof battens

The dimensions of the battens depend on the weight of the covering and the rafter spacing. The following longitudinal cross sections are recommended for average covering: up to 30 cm between rafters -> 24/48 mm battens; 80 cm between rafters -> 30/50 mm battens; 100 cm between

Fig.25:
Roof coverings using under-and-over tiles

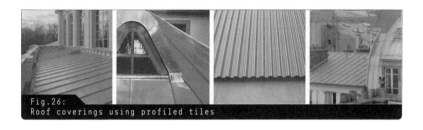
Fig.26:
Roof coverings using profiled tiles

rafters -> 40/60 mm battens. The quality grading of the timber should also be taken into account.

Calculating
spacing between
rafters
The horizontal spacing between the rafters depends on the roof pitch and the choice of roof covering elements. Different values apply according to manufacturer and product. The length of the area to be covered must first be established. It is roughly equivalent to the length of the rafters. The bottom edge of the roof is a special case. The planner must decide, in relation to the structure as a whole, whether the last row of roof tiles should project beyond the ends of the rafters, finish flush or even conclude with an upward tilt. The usual choice is an overhang, corresponding with the overlapping tile area. This is defined as the <u>undereaves course dimension</u>. At the ridge, the covering overlap on the roof batten requires a space to be kept free. This is defined as the <u>ridge course dimension</u>. To calculate the number of rows needed and the resulting space between the battens, the ridge and undereaves course dimensions must be subtracted from the overall length to be covered. The remaining length is divided into equal spacings with a tile overlap as prescribed by the manufacturer.

The number of tile elements needed for the breadth of the roof is also calculated on the basis of the manufacturer's approved dimensions. Here, too, the spacing can very slightly to allow for tolerances and insertions such as chimneys or pipes.

Fig.27:
Roof battens

Table 2:
Roof batten cross sections

Batten cross sections in mm	Axis width in m	DIN 4074 timber grades
24/48	up to 0.70	S 13
24/60	up to 0.80	S 13
30/50	up to 0.80	S 10
40/60	up to 1.00	S 10

A statical examination should be conducted for all other spacings between rafters or batten cross sections.

Cross battens

Cross battens are needed where there are flat tile underlays, or for roof pitches of less than 22°. The same applies to intermediate roof coverings or support systems › see chapter Waterproofing where moisture cannot drain off freely.

\\Example:
Specimen roof batten spacing calculation:
Overall length to be covered: 7.08 m
Undereaves course: 32 cm (to be established)
Ridge course: 4 cm (according to manufacturer's instructions)
Length to be divided: 7.08 m – 0.32 m – 0.04 m = 6.72 m
Average batten spacing according to manufacturer's instructions: 0.33 m
6.72 m : 0.33 m = 20.4 rows
Number of rows selected: 20 rows
It is necessary to check whether the chosen batten spacing of 0.33 m lies within the manufacturer's permitted parameters for the particular roof pitch.

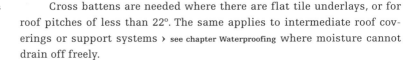

\\Tip:
Cross battens are not absolutely essential with underlays. In such cases the underlay is fitted with a slight sag, so that any water that may penetrate can drain off safely under the roof battens. Even here, cross-battening is recommended, as most underlays shrink over time, and so the material stretches.

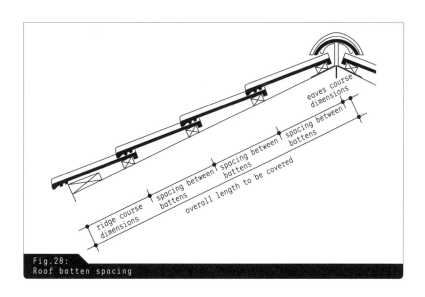

Fig.28:
Roof batten spacing

Waterproofing

The roof covering usually ensures that the roof is rainproof. However, in particularly acute situations, additional planning measures should be taken to obviate spray penetration in cases of high wind or driven snow. Acute situations can be caused by an unduly low roof pitch, highly structured roof surfaces, special roof forms, the adaptation of the roof for living space etc. Special climatic conditions can also make additional measures necessary; for example an exposed position, or areas subject to high winds or frequent heavy snow.

Underlay

The simplest additional element is an underlay. This is fitted as a ventilated sheet structure, i.e. the sheeting is not supported below, but hangs freely between the rafters. Underlay is supplied in rolls, and is usually in the form of reinforced plastic sheeting.

Supported layer

Here the sheets are laid over a support, such as a timber structure. Different qualities are achieved through the nature of the seams. Such supported layers are classed as rainproof. They are fitted below the battens and counter battens.

Sewn welded underlays

These consist of waterproofing sheets joined by welding or gluing to make them waterproof. We distinguish between rainproof and waterproof underlay. A rainproof underlay may include structurally required apertures. The sheets are positioned under the battens and cross battens. No

35

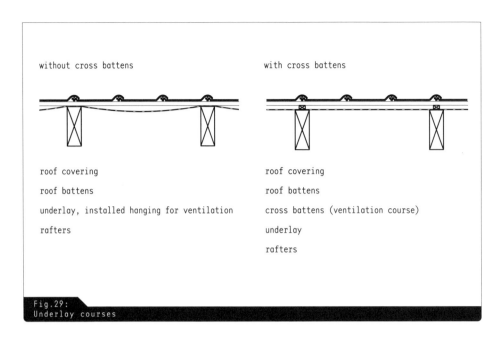

without cross battens

with cross battens

roof covering

roof battens

underlay, installed hanging for ventilation

rafters

roof covering

roof battens

cross battens (ventilation course)

underlay

rafters

Fig.29:
Underlay courses

Table 3:
Extra requirements for roof coverings

Roof pitch	Special requirements relating to use, structure or climate			
	No special requirements	One additional requirement	Two additional requirements	Three additional requirements
> standard roof pitch	–	Underlay	Underlay	Supported overlapping course
> 6° below standard roof pitch	Underlay	Underlay	Supported overlapping course	Separate welded / glued course
> 10° below standard roof pitch	Rainproof underlay	Rainproof underlay	Rainproof underlay	Waterproof underlay
< 10° below standard roof pitch	Rainproof underlay	Waterproof underlay	Waterproof underlay	Waterproof underlay

apertures are permitted in a waterproof underlay. The counter battens are an integral part, i.e. the sheets are fitted between the battens and counter battens. Close attention must be paid when fitting to ensure that water accumulating on the sheets can drain away into the gutter at the eaves. Adequate ventilation must be provided in the roof space under the underlay.

Insulation

If roof spaces are ventilated and not used as living space, the building below is usually insulated on or under the last ceiling. This saves insulation material, in contrast with an insulated roof, and is easier to install. However, roof spaces are increasingly being developed to take advantage of the additional space they can provide. In such cases the roof is included in the heated area of the house and all the structural elements enclosing the used section must meet the appropriate thermal insulation standards.

 > see Appendix

It is important to ensure that the insulation course joins with the exterior wall insulation course, to avoid cold bridges. > see Fig. 31

Thermal insulation

Mineral wool, rigid polystyrene foam boards (PS), rigid polyurethane foam sheeting (PUR), cork, lightweight wood wool sheets and pouring-type granular insulation material are available for thermal insulation. The individual insulation materials are offered with different thermal conductivity ratings. Insulating materials with particularly poor thermal conductivity insulate correspondingly well, and can be thinner than materials with good conductivity, while still providing the same level of insulation. Thermal conductivity, the transmission constant (k), is given in watts per square metre Kelvin (W/m^{2}K). The lower the value, the better the insulating properties.

Thermal insulation can be fitted between the rafters, which must be high enough to provide a sufficiently thick insulation course. A higher rafter than statically necessary to provide the necessary space may be selected, or an additional insulating course can be fitted to the rafters from inside the space. The timber used for the rafters is such a poor conductor

---

\\Hint:
Thermal bridges are particular points in the structure where the building's insulation course is interrupted. Here heat can penetrate the building when there are temperature differences between inside and outside (summer conditions), or it can escape (winter conditions). Situations of this kind should be avoided where possible as water may condense on cold surfaces when the air cools, be trapped inside the structure and damage it.

\\Tip:
Most insulating materials are available in widths to match the most common spacing between rafters, so information about products should be gathered at an early planning stage. It is recommended that the distance between the rafters be fixed according to the gap required, rather than by an even unit spacing.

Fig.30:
Thermal insulation of pitched roofs

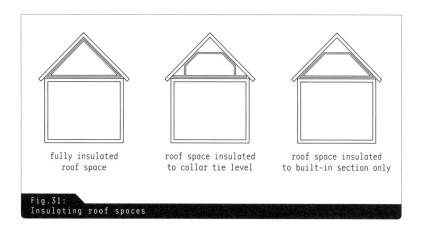

fully insulated
roof space

roof space insulated
to collar tie level

roof space insulated
to built-in section only

Fig.31:
Insulating roof spaces

that thermal bridges are not created even if the insulating course is interrupted.

Insulation
between rafters

Insulation between rafters means that there is an air space between the thermal insulation course and the underlay sheeting, to ventilate the structure. If the height of the rafters is exactly the same as the thickness of the insulating material, the term full rafter insulation is used. If the rafters are to remain visible on the inside, the insulation can be fitted to the roof on the outside, with boarding, as insulation on rafters.

Full rafter
insulation
Insulation on
rafters

Vapour barrier

A vapour barrier is essential for thermally insulated roofs. It is always positioned on the inside of the space, below the thermal insulation. It must cover the full area, and be attached at the edges in such a way that it is airtight. Vapour barriers prevent moisture in the air inside the space from penetrating the thermal insulation or the roof structure through diffusion.

The appropriate insulation rating for the vapour barrier sheeting is determined according to the roof pitch and the length of the rafters. The

\\Hint:

Any air from inside the space that might
diffuse through the thermal insulation would
cool down as it passes from the inside to the
outside (in winter). As warm air contains
more moisture than cold air, water could
condense, making the thermal insulation and
the structure damp, and thus damaging the
building.
If several vapour barriers are fitted inside
part of a building, the outermost in each case
must be more permeable to water vapour than
the inner barriers. Any moisture that may
accumulate can thus escape to the outside.

\\Tip:

Solid building materials can be used instead
of vapour barriers, provided they render
the insulation airtight in relation to the
interior space. These can be OSB boards
(Oriented Strand Boards), for example, with
their joints sealed so that they are airtight
(using appropriate adhesive tapes). Evidence
of effectiveness is usually required here.

vapour insulation rating gives the equivalent diffused air space depth (s_d) for the layer of air. This measures the resistance the material offers to water vapour transmission. Vapour barriers can be fitted in elastomer sheeting or in plastic versions.

To sum up: the structure, and the thermal insulation course in particular, must be protected against water penetration. This is achieved on the inside by fitting vapour barriers, which prevent penetration by moisture in the air. Outside, moisture in the air can evaporate above the ridge underlay or through the roof covering. Any water that may accumulate is drained into the gutters via the underlay sheeting.

TYPES OF FINISH

Unventilated
roof structure

Unventilated roof structures are constructed with full rafter insulation. The insulation is fitted between the vapour barrier (on the inside) and the underlay (on the outside). Counter battens should be placed on top of the underlay, to ensure that any moisture that may penetrate into the gap can evaporate under the roof covering. This construction method is used when the structural elements must be kept as thin as possible, or when a roof is having a structure inserted subsequently, and there is insufficient rafter height for a ventilated structure. But if ventilation for the thermal insulation is considered essential, the rafters can be doubled by fitting an additional lath to the rafters from the outside or by installing a second thermal insulation course inside.

> 🛈

If this approach is used, air is able to circulate below the underlay (roof membrane). The advantage is that any moisture present can evaporate from the insulation material and escape via the ridge joint. The air space also means that the less heat is absorbed into the roof space (in summer). The warm air rises and escapes through the ventilation apertures in the ridge. A suction effect is produced, as in a chimney. It is essential here that sufficient air can flow in through apertures in the eaves.

When planning the air space depth, care should be taken not to fit the insulation completely flat, so that it has room to swell subsequently. If the air is to circulate freely, it must be diverted around trimmers, roof windows, chimneys or dormers, so counter battens should be fitted, enabling air to circulate between the eaves and the ridge. > see Fig. 29

Structures with supported thermal insulation are not usually ventilated. Instead, the roof is covered with prefabricated elements supported by falsework above the rafters. Prefabricated elements of this kind are usually supplied with a vapour barrier on the underside. As in full rafter insulation, the underlay or an appropriate material for draining water away is fitted directly on top of the thermal insulation. This finish reduces building time. The rafters can remain visible underneath, and be used as a design element. In this case the rafters should be finished with planed facing timbers, or with laminated timbers.

The internal surfaces of developed roof spaces should be clad with a material that can absorb moisture and release it again, to produce a pleasant atmosphere in the space. Wall rendering usually performs this function in spaces with masonry walls. Plasterboard sheets are customarily

---

🛈

\\ Hint:
The ventilation cross sections for a ventilated roof structure should correspond to the following minimal values: for roof pitches of more than 10°, 2‰ of the roof area at the eaves, but at least 200 cm², and 5‰ of the roof area at the ridge. The free ventilation cross section must be at least 2 cm (air space depth). For roof pitches of less than 10° the ventilation cross section must be 2‰ of the total roof area at two opposite eaves. The free ventilation cross section must be at least 5 cm. Precise specifications can be found in national standards.

insulation between rafters

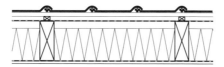

roof covering
battens
counter battens
underlay
air space
thermal insulation
vapour barrier

insulation between rafters with
additional internal insulation

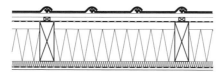

roof covering
battens
counter battens
underlay
air space
thermal insulation
vapour barrier

full rafter insulation

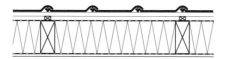

roof covering
battens
counter battens
underlay
thermal insulation
vapour barrier

insulation on rafters

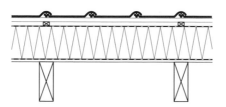

roof covering
battens
counter battens
underlay
air space
thermal insulation
vapour barrier
falsework

Fig.32:
Types of structures for pitched roofs

used for building inside the roof space. They are easy to work and adapt on the building site. Note here that slight movements in the structure can easily produce cracks. Another common wall cladding is produced using matchboard with tongue and groove. This will not crack easily, because the boards can shift in relation to each other. But in most cases the principal deciding factor when choosing interior wall cladding is appearance.

DRAINAGE

Pitched roofs are drained towards the eaves via the roof surfaces and valleys. The precipitation water collects in gutters there, and is taken into the sewerage system via downpipes. The term combined system is used when the water feeds into the public sewerage grid, and separate system when the precipitation feeds into the local groundwater.

Dimensioning

The assumed local rainfall load must be ascertained in order to dimension the gutters and pipes.

The rainfall is calculated from the local rainfall load – generally at 300 litres per second per hectare ($r = 300l/(s*ha)$) – the runoff coefficient, which takes the roof pitch and the nature of the surface into consideration, and the base roof area.

The calculation uses the formula

rainwater runoff ar (in l/s) = runoff coefficient × precipitation area serves r (in m^2) × design rainfall load.

The value produced can then be used to select the appropriate downpipe from standards tables.

Gutters

Gutters are fitted to the eaves with height-adjustable gutter brackets. One bracket per rafter is fitted for timber roof structures, but the brackets

Table 4:
Runoff coefficients (extract from DIN 1986-2 Table 16 / ISO 1438)

Surface types	Runoff coefficient
Surfaces impermeable to water	1.0
Roofs with a pitch of <3°	0.8
Gravel roofs	0.5
Green roofs	0.3
Extensive green roof (d > 10cm)	0.5

Table 5:
Precipitation areas that can be attached to rainwater downpipes of minimum pitch with precipitation quantities of 300 l/(s*ha) according to DIN 1986-2 Table 17 / ISO 1438

Roof pitch	Maximum admissible	Runoff coefficient 1.0	Runoff coefficient 0.8	Runoff coefficient 0.5
	ar in l/s	r in m^2	r in m^2	r in m^2
50	0.7	24	30	48
60	1.2	40	49	79
70	1.8	60	75	120
80	2.6	86	107	171
100	4.7	156	195	312
120	7.6	253	317	507
125	8.5	283	353	565
150	13.8	459	574	918
200	29.6	986	1233	1972

Table 6:
Design for downpipes and gutter assignment (here for PVC) according to DIN 18 461 Table 2 / ISO 1438

Roof area to be attached at a maximum rainfall load of 300 l/(s*ha)	Rainwater runoff	Rainwater downpipes (nominal dimension)	Gutter assigned (nominal value)
in m^2	in l/s	in mm	
20	0.6	50	80
37	1.1	63	80
57	1.7	70	100
97	2.9	90	125
170	5.1	100	150
243	7.3	125	180
483	14.5	150	250

should never be further than 90 cm apart, depending on the structure. The gutters are laid in the gutter brackets. Care should be taken here that the gutter slopes outwards, i.e. that it is higher on the building side than on the outside. Any water that may overflow is thus directed away from the building. The gutter should slope (minimum 2%) towards the drainpipes. Metal gutters in particular expand or contract if temperatures vary, so lengths of 15 m should not be exceeded. Individual gutter sections are joined using connectors. Stop ends are fitted at the ends of the gutters to seal them off.

Downpipes
Gutters have prefabricated joints to which the downpipes are attached with elbows. Sections of pipe are connected by waterproofing and connecting sockets. The pipes are attached to the building by brackets with pins or screws. The pipe should clear the building by more than 20 mm so that damp will not penetrate the wall if the pipe is damaged.

Gutters and pipes can be either angled or round. Various materials are available. Care should be taken that the materials cannot interact with each other to produce corrosion, for example, or create tension as a result of different expansion properties. So, for example, copper gutters and pipes can be assembled only with copper-clad steel brackets and clips. Brackets in galvanized steel or aluminium are recommended for aluminium gutters. Galvanized steel brackets and clips are available for zinc or galvanized steel gutters. PVC gutters can be fitted with galvanized steel or plastic-clad brackets.

It is also recommended that foliage interception grids be fitted to the gutters. These are supplied in the form of longitudinal baskets curving outwards, and increase cleaning intervals. Heated guttering can be installed at awkward places, such as rising structural elements around an internal gutter › see Hint page 63; these will guarantee that water will drain off even in case of snow.

Internal
guttering
Internal guttering is the term used for gutters that are not suspended from the eaves, but positioned above the floor slab. › see Fig. 33 left This design

---

◊

\\ Hint:
Local authorities can supply values for
areas with heavy or light precipitation. An
additional 100% safety element should allowed
for internal gutters.

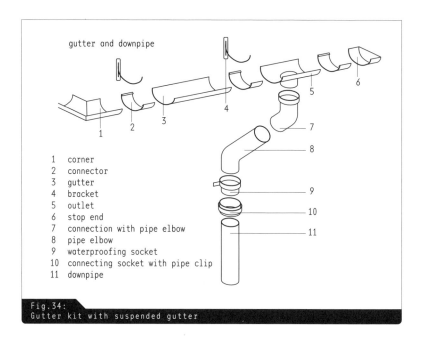

gutter and downpipe

1 corner
2 connector
3 gutter
4 bracket
5 outlet
6 stop end
7 connection with pipe elbow
8 pipe elbow
9 waterproofing socket
10 connecting socket with pipe clip
11 downpipe

Fig.34:
Gutter kit with suspended gutter

is chosen if a roof overhang is not desired or not admissible. A safety gutter can be included so that even if it leaks, water cannot penetrate the building. This can take the form of a waterproofing strip under the metal or plastic gutter. An emergency overflow spout can also be provided.

PRESENTATION

Buildings are presented as drawings in plan views, sections, elevations and details. When drawing a plan view, a notional section is taken at a certain level (usually at 1 to 1.5 m above the finished floor of a particular

\\ Hint:
Individual dimension units are particularly important for working plans. Building dimensions and structural element lengths are usually given in metres (in centimetres for smaller dimensions where appropriate). Dimension chains are compiled in metres or centimetres. Structural element cross sections are given in centimetres. Steel structural elements are dimensioned in millimetres.

storey), so only the structural elements below this are shown. It is therefore often difficult to provide adequate details of the roof structure.

Rafter plans   For the above reason, a rafter plan is usually prepared for pitched roofs. It shows all the wooden structural elements (or the corresponding features for other structures) as a top view. The roof covering, waterproofing, internal cladding etc. are not shown. The plan is used as a working guide by the on-site carpenters. In order to define the position of the roof structure, also called roof truss, in the building, the topmost floor slab must also be shown (unbroken line for visible structural element), along with the walls below (dashed line for concealed structural element), and a dimensional reference to the roof. If structural elements such as supports, stays or angle braces are concealed by the rafters above them, they are shown as dashed lines. The roof battens and counter battens are not shown, even though they are timber structures, because they will be later fitted by the roofers, not the carpenters. All the different wooden parts are allocated a position number, which is usually entered on the plan as a circled number, with a line or arrow to connect it to the particular structural element. A legend then describes the structural elements. Information must be given about the dimensions (width times height of cross section) and grade of the building material.

Information about installation or connections should also be recorded. The structural elements are dimensioned by the architect, structural designer or structural engineer.

In addition to the rafter plan, the following details should be provided for the building work, with drawings of all the layers of structural elements: ridge joint, eaves, verge, penetrations, apertures, and all special solutions.

\\ Hint:
The dimensions of the wooden structural elements are usually given as cross sections. A beam with a rectangular cross section of 10 cm x 12 cm is defined as 10/12, spoken as "ten to twelve". Round parts are defined by their diameter, and steel parts by their product or profile designation (e.g. HEA 120, U 100 etc.). Length and position are fixed according to the dimensions in the plan.

\\ Hint:
Further information about drawings can be found in "Basics Technical Drawing" by Bert Bielefeld and Isabella Skiba, published by Birkhäuser Publishers, Basel 2007

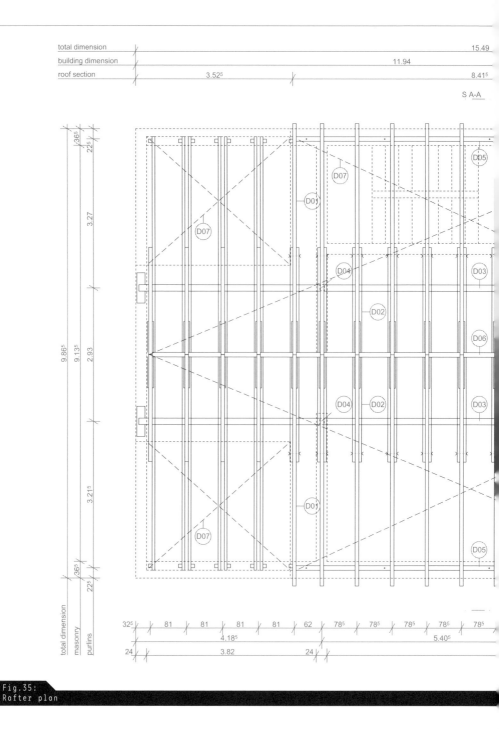

total dimension   15.49
building dimension   11.94
roof section   3.52⁵   8.41⁵

S A-A

Fig.35:
Rafter plan

48

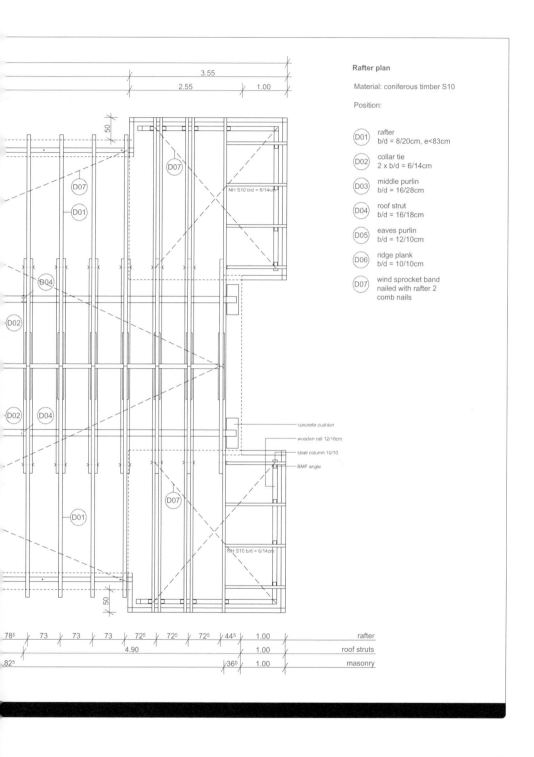

Rafter plan

Material: coniferous timber S10

Position:

(D01)	rafter	b/d = 8/20cm, e<83cm
(D02)	collar tie	2 x b/d = 6/14cm
(D03)	middle purlin	b/d = 16/28cm
(D04)	roof strut	b/d = 16/18cm
(D05)	eaves purlin	b/d = 12/10cm
(D06)	ridge plank	b/d = 10/10cm
(D07)	wind sprocket band	nailed with rafter 2 comb nails

Dimensions / labels within drawing:

3.55
2.55   1.00
50
NH S10 b/d = 6/14cm
concrete cushion
wooden rail 12/16cm
steel column 10/10
BMF angle
NH S10 b/d = 6/14cm
50

78⁵	73	73	73	72⁵	72⁵	72⁵	44⁵	1.00	rafter
4.90								1.00	roof struts
82⁵							36⁵	1.00	masonry

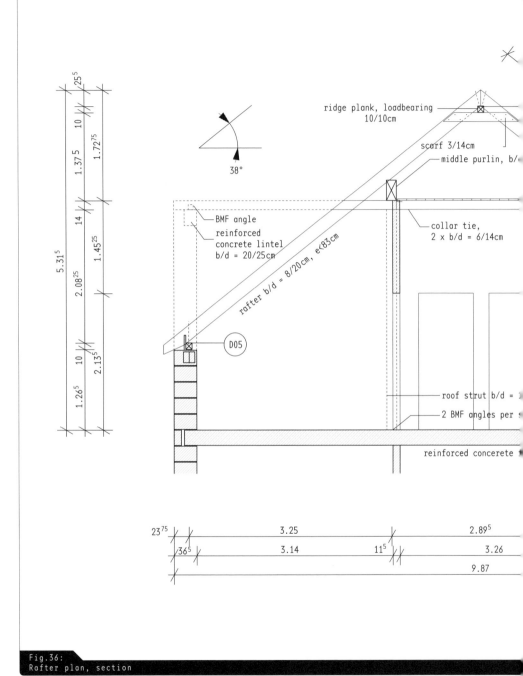

ridge plank, loadbearing 10/10cm

scarf 3/14cm

middle purlin, b/

38°

BMF angle
reinforced
concrete lintel
b/d = 20/25cm

collar tie,
2 x b/d = 6/14cm

rafter b/d = 8/20cm, e⊄83cm

D05

roof strut b/d = 1

2 BMF angles per s

reinforced concerete

5.31⁵

25⁵
10
1.37⁵
14
2.08²⁵
10
1.26⁵

1.72⁷⁵
1.45²⁵
2.13⁵

23⁷⁵   3.25   2.89⁵
/36⁵   3.14   11⁵   3.26
9.87

Fig.36:
Rafter plan, section

50

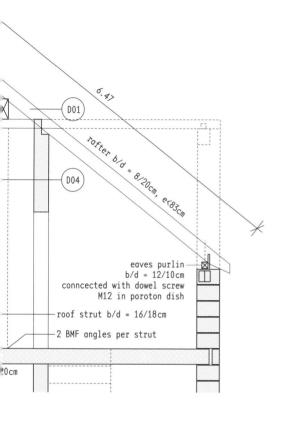

6.47

rafter b/d = 8/20cm, e<83cm

D01

D04

eaves purlin
b/d = 12/10cm
conncected with dowel screw
M12 in poroton dish

roof strut b/d = 16/18cm

2 BMF angles per strut

0cm

3.25   23^{75}

24   2.38^5 36^5

SECTION A-A

Material: coniferous timber S10

Positions:

D01	rafter b/d = 8/20cm, e<83cm
D02	collar tie 2 x b/d = 6/14cm
D03	middle purlin b/d = 16/28cm
D04	roof strut b/d = 16/18cm
D05	eaves purlin b/d = 12/10cm
D06	ridge plank b/d = 10/10cm
D07	wind sprocket band nailed with rafter 2 comb nails

Table 7:
Summary of structural elements for pitched roofs

Structural elements	Illustrations	Hints	Usual dimensions for average roofs
Eaves board		For couple roofs	8/12–10/22
Tie beam		For couple roofs	12/12–14/14
Ridge purlin		On walls or posts	14/16–16/22
Eaves purlin		On the ceiling or external wall	10/10–14/16
Collar tie		Usually in the form of a binding tie	8/14–10/20
Collar rafter		Internal curb	8/14–8/22
Angle clip		For tie bars	
Angle brace ties		Strut on post in longitudinal direction	10/10–10/12
Middle purlin		Under the rafters	12/20–14/20

Structural element	Illustration	Hints	Usual dimensions for average roofs
Post		Supports purlins	12/12–14/14
Guide member		For simple assembly	Thicknesses from 22 mm
Rafter		Supports roof covering	8/14–8/22
Brace		For transverse reinforcements	14/16
Verge member		For couple roof	Length 20 cm
Trimmer		For apertures	8/14–8/22
Sprocket		Reinforcement	In flat steel
Binding tie		Horizontal reinforcement, in pairs	6/14–8/16

FLAT ROOFS

BASICS

A flat roof has a pitch of less than 5°. However, flat roof structures are suitable for shallow-pitch roofs (up to 25°), although here the building materials must be adequately protected against slippage. The top section of a flat roof is the roof covering, known as the roof weatherproofing or waterproofing. Flat roofs can be constructed to support people or vehicles. For example, the space on the roof can be used as a terrace, parking deck or for fitting ventilation equipment. The roof surface must be carefully planned: seen from the neighbouring buildings the roof is the fifth façade, and is therefore important in terms of the building's appearance as well. Like pitched roofs, flat roofs have to meet various requirements. They must provide adequate protection against moisture and precipitation, as well as against heat, cold and wind. They must transfer the forces exerted by their self-weight, snow and traffic safely into the structure below them. Wind suction has an important part to play as a load, as the materials used to waterproof the roof are usually light, and thus have to be secured against lifting and mechanical movements.

Flat roofs can be finished flush with the walls, or they can protrude. The upturn at the edge of the roof is known as the roof parapet. It is where the insulating and waterproofing elements of the roof are brought together. Precipitation is usually drained into the interior of the building and thus directed from the edge of the roof towards the roof outlets. An incline of at least 2% must be guaranteed.

LAYERS OF STRUCTURAL ELEMENTS

Flat roofs can have various functional layers, which must be matched to each other. It is essential that the layer sequence provide adequate insulation against heat and noise.

> 🔖

🔖

\\ Hint:
Evidence about heat and noise insulation for
the whole building, according to the building
type, is part of the planning permission
process with the responsible building
department.

The moisture to which the structural layers are exposed (e.g. trapped humidity, condensation build-up) must be able to escape. Building materials must be compatible with each other.

The course below the waterproofing, which deals with water, is called the undercourse. It can be the loadbearing structure, e.g. a concrete surface, or also boarding or the thermal insulation component. It is important that the waterproofing material match the undercourse, to avoid expansion cracks, for example. Joints between prefabricated parts must be covered by separator strips at least 20 cm wide.

Bonding courses are installed to improve the adhesive properties of building component layers. These can be primers or prior applications of bitumen solutions and bitumen emulsions. Bonding courses are painted, rolled or sprayed onto a clean undercourse.

If layers of components turn out to be uneven or rough, a levelling course may be needed. This compensates for component tolerances, creates a smooth surface and is supplied as bitumen roofing sheet, glass or plastic fleece, and as foam mats. It is laid loose or spot-glued.

Separating layers or courses are laid to ensure that adjacent layers of structural elements with different expansion properties can move in relation to each other, or to accommodate other mechanical movements. They can also be used if two materials are chemically incompatible. The same materials can be used as for the levelling courses.

Vapour barriers are used to regulate moisture transmission inside the building. › see chapter Pitched roofs, Types of finish They are not waterproof, but simply inhibit vapour diffusion. The inhibition factor indicates how much moisture can diffuse through the vapour barrier. They can be bitumen roofing sheets, plastic vapour inhibiting sheets, elastomer roofing sheets, or compound foils. They can be laid loose or spot-glued. Points at which the individual sheets meet must be fully glued. The vapour barrier must extend to the top edge of the insulating course and be fixed there at roof edges and at penetrations. Vapour barriers can also be used to ensure that a roof is airtight.

Thermal insulation protects the building from heat loss in summer, and prevents large thermal build-ups through insolation in summer (summer thermal insulation). Expanded polystyrene (EPS), extruded polystyrene foam (XPS), extruded polyurethane (PUR), mineral fibre insulating material (MF), foam glass (FG), cork, wood fibre insulation material, or expanded

\\ Hint:
All roof areas must be built with a slope
of at least 2% to the roof outlets. If the
roof structure itself does not slope, a slope
can be created with sloping screed (laid on
the roof slab with a separating course) or
with sloping insulation. The key feature
in deciding between the two possibilities,
after the question of expense, is whether
the structure can take the additional weight
of the screed or whether the insulation is
available in appropriate thicknesses.

\\ Tip:
If the slope is created with insulation
wedges, the individual insulated areas meet at
an angle of 45° for rectangular floor plans. A
valley is created at the joint. For the valley
to have a 2% slope, the insulation wedges must
have a 3% slope.

bituminized mineral infill may be used. If the thermal insulation is laid above the waterproofing course, care should be taken that all the subsequent courses be permeable to vapour diffusion, so that any moisture can escape. The thermal insulation can also be used to create a roof drainage incline. These insulation materials are supplied in an appropriate form by the manufacturer and are known as gradient insulation. Single elements are called insulation wedges.

Sheet insulation should be laid with an offset and joints that are as tight as possible. The insulation is glued to the surface below and the sheets are attached to each other according to the manufacturer's instructions.

Vapour pressure compensation course

A vapour pressure compensation course is fitted to distribute the water vapour pressure evenly in the roof waterproofing material. Such layers, like vapour barriers, may consist of bitumen roof sheeting, plastic vapour barrier sheeting, elastomer roof sheeting or compound foils. They are laid loose or spot-glued.

Roof waterproofing

The water-bearing course is created by the roof waterproofing. It is a closed, waterproof area and can be produced with bitumen roof sheeting, plastic or elastomer roof sheeting or fluid-applied waterproofing. Bitumen sheet waterproofing should have at least two layers. It must be laid with an overlap of at least 80 mm and be glued along the full area of the joints. Plastic or elastomer sheeting is applied in one layer. It must be glued over the full area. The overlap must be at least 40 mm. Fluid-applied waterproofing is laid in one layer. It must be applied so that it adheres over the full area. A separating course should be used if the course underneath is

open, for example for sheet insulation or a timber frame. The waterproofing must be at least 1.5 mm thick, at least 2 mm for used roofs.

Filter course

A protective or filter course is used to protect the waterproofing from mechanical influences. PVC, rubber or plastic granulate highly perforation-proof sheets, drainage mats or sheets of extruded polystyrene foam are used.

Surface protection

Modern foil roofs are installed as single-layer waterproofing courses and attached to the course below with strips that are glued on subsequently, or spot-attached. They are usually made of light-coloured materials, so that thermal expansion as a result of sunlight is minimized. Because of their material properties they offer adequate protection from UV radiation. No additional surface protection need be used for foil roofs. This saves weight, and the roof structure can be designed with less self-weight. Surface protection is applied if the roof waterproofing does not provide adequate protection against UV radiation, wind upthrust or mechanical loads. A light surface protection is provided for bitumen sheets according to load. This can be achieved by applying sand, for example. Crushed slate is sprinkled into a cold polymer bitumen compound and attached to the bitumen sheeting.

Gravel surface protection courses are known as heavy surface protection. The gravel layer should be at least 50 mm thick when installed. The weight of the stones can prevent unfixed roof coverings being lifted by wind suction. If the surface is protected with crushed stone or gravel, care should be taken that the grain size be sufficient for the material not to blow away in the wind. A sheet covering is preferable for surfaces exposed to strong winds.

Accessible coverings

Accessible coverings, i.e. coverings that can be walked on, can also be used to protect the surface. In such cases a compression-resistant thermal

58

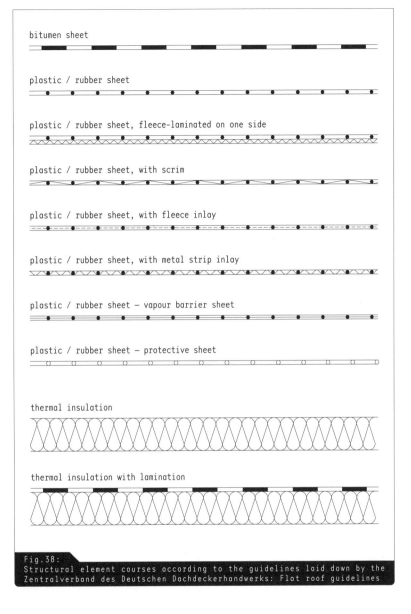

bitumen sheet

plastic / rubber sheet

plastic / rubber sheet, fleece-laminated on one side

plastic / rubber sheet, with scrim

plastic / rubber sheet, with fleece inlay

plastic / rubber sheet, with metal strip inlay

plastic / rubber sheet – vapour barrier sheet

plastic / rubber sheet – protective sheet

thermal insulation

thermal insulation with lamination

Fig.38:
Structural element courses according to the guidelines laid down by the
Zentralverband des Deutschen Dachdeckerhandwerks: Flat roof guidelines

insulation course should be installed. The roof waterproofing must be adequately protected against mechanical influences.

If the joints between the slabs are sealed, or the entire covering is closed, a slope of at least 1% must be created. Drainage is then maintained on the waterproofing, and it becomes the water-bearing course. The slabs chosen must be frostproof. Expansion joints should be provided to allow for thermal expansion. Sufficient spacing should be maintained at the edges to prevent the raised waterproofing from damage. Accessible coverings can be laid in the form of small slabs in a bed of mortar on a tufted mat or a drainage course. The mortar bed should be approx. 4 cm thick. Spot bedding is recommended for larger slab coverings. Prefabricated height-adjustable elements can compensate for tolerances here. Compression-proof thermal insulation, such as foam glass, should be used to prevent the adjustable elements punching holes in the roof waterproofing. A more simple method is to lay the covering on little bags of mortar. For this, fresh mortar is packed into little plastic sacks and placed under the corners of the slabs. Once the slabs are resting on the mortar sacks, they can be levelled to compact the mortar completely. The cavity under the slabs is maintained and the slabs are not bedded directly on the waterproofing. Large slabs should be laid in a bed of gravel for better weight distribution. Here the gravel bed is approx. 5 cm thick. The gravel selected should allow any accumulated precipitation water to drain off freely.

Green roof

Plants can also be used to protect the surface. Here we distinguish, according to the thickness of the course and the plants chosen, between extensive and intensive planting. The additional load exerted on the roof should be considered at the structural calculation stage. Note also when choosing waterproofing that it must not be compromised by the roots, or a special root course should be installed. For extensive planting, the slope may be omitted to ensure that sufficient water is available for the plants. But care must be taken if damage does occur that water cannot seep through the whole set of courses. The individual waterproofing courses should be glued and divided into several fields by bulkhead-style barriers. These are placed vertically, and split the roof into several areas that are then drained separately. <u>Leaks are easier to locate.</u>

TYPES OF FINISH

We distinguish between three different principles for flat roof structures or course layers.

Unventilated roof

An unventilated roof (previously called a warm roof) has its waterproofing course on the outside and so the thermal insulation is in the sealed "warm area". A typical structure for an unventilated roof involves applying a preparatory coating to prepare the surface of the roof structure, which may be in reinforced concrete roof, steel or wood. The levelling course and the vapour barrier are laid on this surface. The insulation is

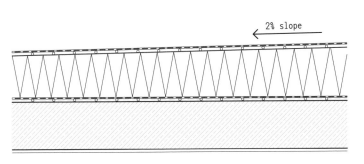

2% slope

roof waterproofing, single course
vapour pressure compensation course
thermal insulation in sloping insulation slabs
vapour barrier
levelling course
preliminary coating
reinforced concrete slab

Fig.39:
Unventilated roof

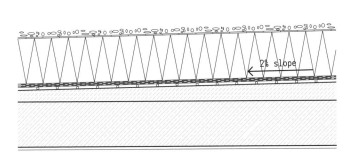

2% slope

surface protection, gravel, min. 5 cm, grain 16–32
filter course
thermal insulation, durable, water resistant
waterproofing courses, 3 layers
levelling course
sloping screed
reinforced concrete slab

Fig.40:
Upside-down roof

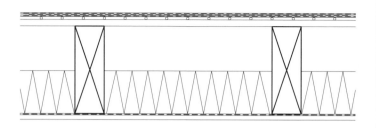

roof waterproofing, three courses
levelling course
boarding substructure 22 mm
air space, min. 15 cm
thermal insulation
rafters
vapour barrier
plasterboard sheet

Fig.41:
Ventilated roof

made of hard-wearing sloping slabs. Here great care must be taken that all areas of the roof drain towards a roof outlet or a gutter, with a slope of at least 2% (3% is better). A vapour pressure compensation course is laid on the insulation, and the waterproofing is applied to this; it can consist of one or more courses. Surface protection should be provided according to the product chosen.

Upside-down roof

The second approach to building up a layer structure is the upside-down roof. It is also called an IRMA roof (Insulated Roof Membrane Assembly). Here the thermal insulation course is above the waterproofing course, and must therefore be made of a water-resistant insulation material. For this structure, a sloping screed with an incline of at least 2% is placed on the roof support structure within the sequence of courses. The roof waterproofing is supported by a levelling course drained by the slope of the screed. The thermal insulation is also installed in the form of flat slabs. A filter course is placed on top to prevent elements of the surface protection material being washed into the insulation.

Ventilated roof

The third construction available is the ventilated roof (formerly also known as a cold roof). Ventilated roofs are often used for timber roof structures. The course structure is such that boarding, e.g. a sheet of plasterboard or chipboard, tops the floor below. A vapour barrier runs under the rafters above it. The thermal insulation is between the rafters, and may consist of a single layer. An air space of at least 15 cm must be left above the thermal insulation, between the rafters, to guarantee adequate through ventilation. Boarding is fitted on top of the rafters; this can consist of chipboard, tongue-and-groove boarding or a similar material. The waterproofing layers are laid on a levelling course. Surfaces can be protected where necessary.

FLASHING

Rising structural elements

To prevent spray or water that has accumulated on the roof from penetrating the structure the waterproofing must be taken higher. Structural elements rising from the roof may include higher sections of the building, lift headgear, chimneys or service spaces. The same waterproofing principles apply to windows and doors. Given a flat roof pitch of up to 5° the waterproofing must be continued and secured at least 15 cm above the top edge of the roof covering on the rising structural element. The top edge of the roof covering is not the waterproofing course, but may be the gravel surface protection. If the roof pitch is greater than 5° the waterproofing must be taken at least 10 cm up the rising structural element.

Door thresholds

Balcony and terrace doors present a particular difficulty. If the waterproofing is taken 15 cm above the working surface of the roof, there will inevitably be a step between the interior and the exterior. In most cases the shell height of the floor is the same inside and out, but the roof structure is much higher than the floor structure inside, because of the high proportion of waterproofing material. This requires an additional

\\ Hint:
Walls or columns standing vertically on the roof are examples of rising structural elements. The roof waterproofing meets a "rising structural element" at these points and must be appropriately secured to ensure that precipitation, spray or condensation water cannot run under the waterproofing course.

offset. But in order to make the roof area easily accessible, the flashing height can be reduced to 5 cm. This should ensure that if water accumulates in snowy conditions it cannot penetrate behind the waterproofing. If there is no roof outlet immediately outside the door, a grating or a gutter should be positioned there. Doors without thresholds may be essential when "barrier-free building" is required, e.g. in public buildings. This involves special construction methods, such as protection against spray by canopies, heated gutters connected directly to the drainage system, or a roof structure with fully bonded courses.

The waterproofing, and where applicable the separating course, can be secured with clamping rails, which are pinned to the rising wall. Plastic waterproofing can be glued to composite metal sheeting. Joints should also be inserted in the rails at points where the building has expansion joints, to avoid tension. The upward run of waterproofing can be masked with canted metal sheets attached to the rails to cover the waterproofing. These extend into the surface covering area. Care should be taken here that the sheet metal not cause mechanical damage to the waterproofing. For curtain façades, the waterproofing should be taken behind the façade, although it is essential that the waterproofing be easily accessible in case of damage.

All components should satisfy the appropriate fireproofing criteria. Care should also be taken in the case of rising parts of the building that a fire could not spread to higher sections through apertures in the roof, such as light cupolas. A gap of 5 m should be maintained to prevent possible flashover.

ROOF EDGING

Projecting flat roof

Flat roofs can be finished as projecting flat roofs at the point where they meet the façade, or with an upstand. Current practice is to finish the roof with a parapet or an edge trim. Projecting flat roofs present structural problems, as the waterproofing and insulating course in the roof and wall sections cannot easily be combined. If the external envelope is to be clad void-free in thermal insulation material, to avoid thermal bridges, the projecting section of the roof must be completely covered with thermal insulation material. This, however, makes it look unduly thick as a structural element. The second possibility is to apply the thermal insulation to the inside of the roof slab, which is not an ideal solution, as it is impossible to make a direct connection with the insulating course in the wall element. This would also place the roof slab structure in the cold outside area, so it would behave differently in relation to

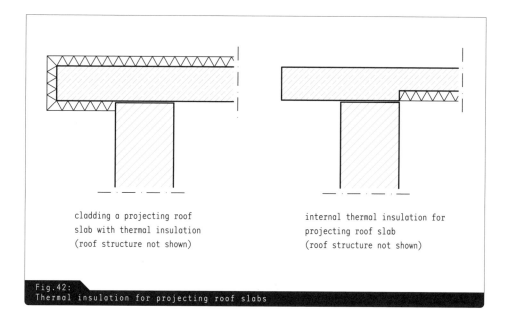

cladding a projecting roof
slab with thermal insulation
(roof structure not shown)

internal thermal insulation for
projecting roof slab
(roof structure not shown)

Fig.42:
Thermal insulation for projecting roof slabs

temperature changes from the loadbearing walls or columns below it.
This could create tension at the connection points, which could cause
cracks in the structure or the façade. This method is often used to provide
existing listed buildings with thermal insulation subsequently, to maintain the appearance of the façade.

Roof parapet,
upstand

For roof edging with upstands the waterproofing layers can be continued upwards, as for the rising structural elements in the flat roof structure. Here, the topmost point should stand at least 10 cm above the roof.
The reference level is the topmost layer – the foil, gravel or working surface. The upstands can be finished as a roof parapet, e.g. in reinforced
concrete or masonry, or with a roof edge trim mounted on an edging plank.
The edging plank is usually a simple rectangular timber that can lie flat on
the plane of the insulation. The roof edge trim is shaped to run around the
edge of the roof and overlap part of the façade. If a roof parapet is chosen,
metal sheeting is usually employed to perform this function, but there are
also prefabricated stone and concrete versions. According to the height of
the building, different dimensional recommendations apply, as the wind
situation becomes more critical with increasing height. The parapet should
project approx. 2 cm over the façade to create a drip edge and prevent any
rainwater that may accumulate from running behind the sheet metal.

roof edge with parapet   roof edge with edge trim

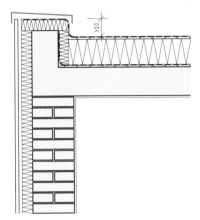 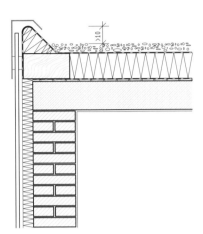

roof structure	wall structure	roof structure	wall structure
roof waterproofing,	façade slabs	gravel course	façade slabs
single course	air space	roof waterproofing,	air space
vapour pressure	thermal insulation	single course	thermal insulation
compensation course	calcium silicate	vapour pressure	calcium silicate
thermal insulation	masonry	compensation course	masonry
vapour barrier		thermal insulation	
levelling course		vapour barrier	
preliminary coating		levelling course	
reinforced concrete slab		preliminary coating	
		reinforced concrete slab	

Fig.43:
Roof edge with parapet and edge trim

Table 8:
Façade overlaps for parapet sheets

Building height	Parapet sheet overlap
< 8 m	5 cm
8–20 m	8 cm
> 20 m	10 cm

DRAINAGE

Flat roofs are usually drained internally, i.e. the downpipes run through the building to the drainage system in the foundations. Every roof must have at least one outlet plus an emergency outlet. The dimensions of the outlet pipes are established as for pitched roofs. > see chapter Pitched roofs, Drainage

Slope

The roof should slope by at least 2% to take the water to the outlets, as it impossible to construct a completely flat roof. The slope prevents puddles from forming. It is created either with a sloping screed or sloping insulation. > see also section Insulation If the rooftop is to be accessible, accumulated precipitation water should be drained away on the surface as well as on the insulation plane. Roof outlets or roof gullies should be arranged so that they are at the lowest point on the roof, and freely accessible. It is possible to install inspection grids, for example, for used rooftops. These should be placed at least 30 cm away from rising structural elements or joints, so that the outlet can be cleanly waterproofed.

Roof outlets

The roof gullies must have a locking waterproofing ring for foils or an adhesive flange, bonded securely with the waterproofing course, for bituminous seals. Gullies for flat roofs are available with both vertical and angled inlets. The vertical version is preferable in principle, as the water is taken directly into the downpipe, and any leaks can be located quickly. Angled flat roof gullies are used when large connected areas are overbuilt, for example, and it is impossible to drain the water off directly (e.g. column-free spaces).

Heating the roof outlets is recommended in areas with heavy snowfall, so that they do not freeze. This ensures drainage in winter as well.

Emergency overflow

To prevent water from accumulating on the roof, when an outlet is blocked with leaves, for example, an emergency overflow must be installed. Emergency overflows are waterspouts running through the roof edging (parapet). They must be placed at a low point of the slope, and be waterproofed and insulated on all sides. The projecting section of the tube must be long enough to prevent water from running down the façade. The water does not have to be directed into the drainage system as an emergency overflow is not a permanent drainage feature.

Fig.44:
Emergency overflow

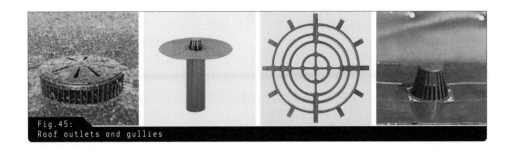

Fig.45:
Roof outlets and gullies

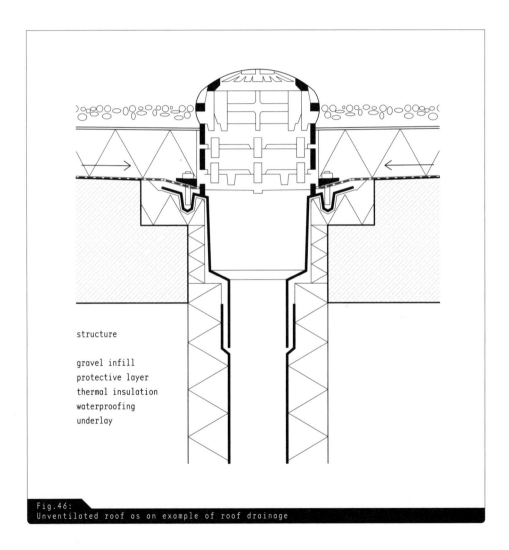

structure

gravel infill
protective layer
thermal insulation
waterproofing
underlay

Fig.46:
Unventilated roof as an example of roof drainage

IN CONCLUSION

The preceding chapters have introduced various roof forms, materials and designs. This book confines itself to simple forms, but it is soon clear that there is no such thing as a standard roof: so many different combinations are possible. Planners must define and fix the layer structure, along with all the connections, conclusions and penetrations. The following points should be borne in mind when working out the details:

Forms:

   _ Is the chosen roof structure compatible with the size and shape of the ground plan?
   _ Are access and a second escape route (e.g. through a window) guaranteed?
   _ Are the chosen roof form and, where applicable, the dormers admissible under the building regulations?
   _ Are the chosen materials suitable for the overall appearance of the building and its surroundings?
   _ Are lighting and ventilation for the roof space guaranteed?

Finish:

   _ Does the building have adequate thermal insulation on all its outside surfaces (gables, dormers, roof surfaces, roof superstructures, pipe runs)?
   _ Is the insulation joined to the insulation layer in adjacent structural elements at all points (walls, balconies etc.)?
   _ Is the roof reliably rainproof?
   _ Can moisture accumulating within a structural element escape?
   _ Can rainwater flow unhindered from all roof surfaces?
   _ Is the roof windproof?
   _ Is condensation (e.g. at penetration points) excluded?
   _ Have precautions been taken against atmospheric moisture penetrating the structure, and particularly the insulation?

Roofs offer great scope for design, in addition to all the conventional forms. New interpretations of familiar structural elements can be exciting features, while reduction to the essentials emphasizes strict order in the overall picture. Despite all the standards and regulations governing building, planners should develop a roof concept first; construction is the second step.

APPENDIX

STANDARDS

Loads and forces	
E DIN 1052	Entwurf, Berechnung und Bemessung von Holzbauwerken – Allgemeine Bemessungsregeln und Bemessungsregeln für den Hochbau, Berlin, Beuth-Verlag 2000 (Design, calculation and dimensioning for timber buildings)
E DIN 1055-1	Einwirkungen auf Tragwerke – Teil 1: Wichte und Flächenlasten von Baustoffen, Bauteilen und Lagerstoffen, Berlin, Beuth-Verlag 2000 (Effect on load-bearing systems, part 1, weights and area loads for materials, parts and stored material)
E DIN 1055-3	Einwirkungen auf Tragwerke – Teil 3: Eigen- und Nutzlasten für Hochbauten, Berlin, Beuth-Verlag 2000 (Work on load-bearing systems, part 3, own weight and imposed loads for building)
E DIN 1055-4	Einwirkungen auf Tragwerke – Teil 4: Windlasten, Berlin, Beuth-Verlag 2001 2001 (Effect on load-bearing systems, part 4, wind loads)
E DIN 1055-5	Einwirkungen auf Tragwerke - Teil 5: Schnee- und Eislasten, Berlin, Beuth-Verlag 2000 (Effect on load-bearing systems, part 5, snow and ice loads)

Sealing	
DIN 18195	Bauwerksabdichtungen, Teile 1-6 und 8-10, Ausgaben 8/83 bis 12/86, Berlin, Beuth-Verlag 1983/1986 (Sealing buildings)

Insulation	
DIN 4108	Beiblatt 2, Wärmeschutz und Energie-Einsparung in Gebäuden. Wärmebrücken. Planungs- und Ausführungsbeispiele (1998-08) (Supplementary sheet 2, heat insulation and energy saving in buildings, heat bridges, examples of planning and execution)
DIN 4108-2	Wärmeschutz und Energie-Einsparung in Gebäuden. Mindestanforderungen an den Wärmeschutz (2001-03) (Heat insulation and energy saving in buildings, minimum demands)

DIN 4108-3	Wärmeschutz und Energie-Einsparung in Gebäuden. Klimabedingter Feuchteschutz, Anforderungen, Berechnungsverfahren und Hinweise für die Planung und Ausführung (2001-07) (Heat insulation and energy saving in buildings, climate-related damp protection, requirements, calculation procedures and hints for planning and execution)
DIN V 4108-4	Wärmeschutz und Energie-Einsparung in Gebäuden. Wärme- und feuchteschutztechnische Bemessungswerte (2002-02) (Heat insulation and energy saving in buildings, heat and damp protection technical dimension values)
DIN 4108-7	Wärmeschutz und Energie-Einsparung in Gebäuden. Luftdichtheit von Gebäuden. Anforderungen, Planungs- und Ausführungsempfehlungen sowie -beispiele (2001-08) (Heat insulation and energy saving in buildings, air-tightness of buildings, requirements, planning and execution recommendations and examples)
SN EN ISO 10211-1	Wärmebrücken im Hochbau – Berechnung der Wärmeströme und Oberflächentemperaturen – Teil 1: Allgemeine Verfahren (ISO 10211-1:1995), 1995 (Heat bridges – calculating heat currents and surface temperatures, part 1, general procedures)
SN EN ISO 10211-2	Wärmebrücken im Hochbau - Berechnung der Wärmeströme und Oberflächentemperaturen - Teil 2: Linienförmige Wärmebrücken (ISO 10211-2:2001), 2001 (Heat bridges – calculating heat currents and surface temperatures, part 2, linear heat bridges)

Drainage

DIN 18460	Regenfallleitungen ausserhalb von Gebäuden und Dachrinnen (Rainfall drainage outside buildings and gutters)
DIN EN 612	Hängedachrinnen, Regenfallrohre ausserhalb von Gebäuden und Zubehörteile aus Metall, Berlin, Beuth-Verlag, 1996 (Suspended roof gutters, drainpipes outside buildings and metal components)
SN EN 612	Hängedachrinnen mit Aussteifung der Rinnenvorderseite und Regenrohre aus Metallblech mit Nahtverbindungen, 2005 (Suspended gutters with reinforced gutter fronts and sheet metal drainpipes with seam joints)
SSIV-10SN EN 12056-3	Schwerkraftentwässerungsanlagen innerhalb von Gebäuden – Teil 3: Dachentwässerung, Planung und Bemessung, Ausgabe 2000 (Gravity drainage inside buildings, part 3, roof drainage, planning and dimensioning)

LITERATURE

Francis D.K. Ching: *Building Construction illustrated*, 3rd edition, John Wiley & Sons, 2004

Andrea Deplazes (ed.): *Constructing Architecture*, Birkhäuser Publishers, Basel 2005

Thomas Herzog, Michael Volz, Julius Natterer, Wolfgang Winter, Roland Schweizer: *Timber Construction Manual*, Birkhäuser Publishers, Basel 2004

Ernst Neufert, Peter Neufert: *Architects' Data*, 3rd edition, Blackwell Science, UK USA Australia 2004

Eberhard Schunck, Hans Jochen Oster, Kurt Kiessl, Rainer Barthel: *Roof Construction Manual*, Birkhäuser Publishers, Basel 2003

Andrew Watts: *Modern Construction Roofs*, Springer Wien New York 2006

Series editor: Bert Bielefeld
Conception: Bert Bielefeld, Annette Gref

Layout and Cover design: Muriel Comby
Translation into English: Michael Robinson
English Copy editing: Monica Buckland

A CIP catalogue record for this book is available
from the Library of Congress, Washington D.C.,
USA

Bibliographic information published by
Die Deutsche Bibliothek
Die Deutsche Bibliothek lists this publication
in the Deutsche Nationalbibliografie; detailed
bibliographic data is available on the
Internet at http://dnb.ddb.de.

This book is also available in a German (ISBN 3-
7643-7682-1) and a French (ISBN 3-7643-7952-9)
language edition.

© 2007 Birkhäuser – Publishers for Architecture,
P.O. Box 133, CH-4010 Basel, Switzerland
Member of Springer Science + Business Media

Printed on acid-free paper produced from
chlorine-free pulp. TCF ∞
Printed in Germany

ISBN-10: 3-7643-7683-X
ISBN-13: 978-3-7643-7683-3

9 8 7 6 5 4 3 2 1   www.birkhauser.ch

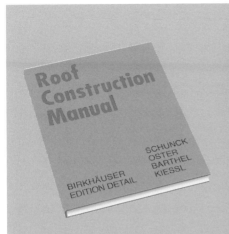